# Animal Helpers
## Zoos

by Jennifer Keats Curtis with
Patti Clark, Jason Fantuzzi, John
Gomes, Robyn Johnson, Patrick Lampi,
Carey Riccardone and Brint Spencer

Only in a zoo can you see rhinos, antelopes, and giraffes of Africa before visiting big polar bears splashing through icy waters.

Zoos are safe, permanent homes for native and exotic animals. Some zoo animals are plentiful in the wild. Others are endangered. People who work in zoos feed and care for wild animals. They may help conserve and protect a whole species. They also teach visitors about these animals and perhaps even what can be done to keep them from becoming extinct.

Would *you* like to
be a zookeeper?

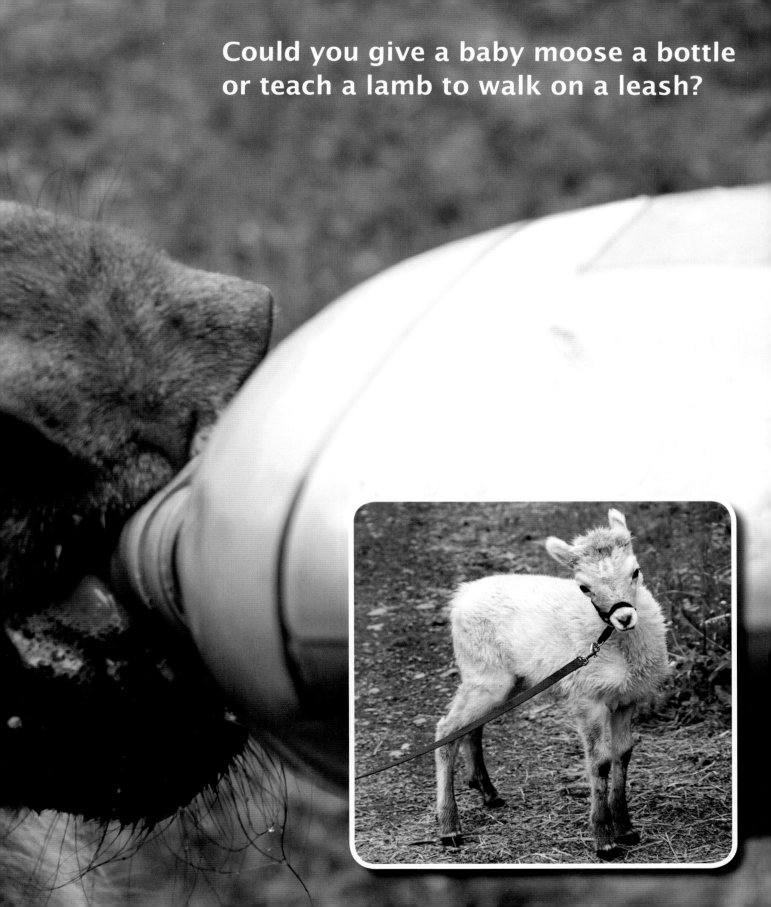

Could you give a baby moose a bottle or teach a lamb to walk on a leash?

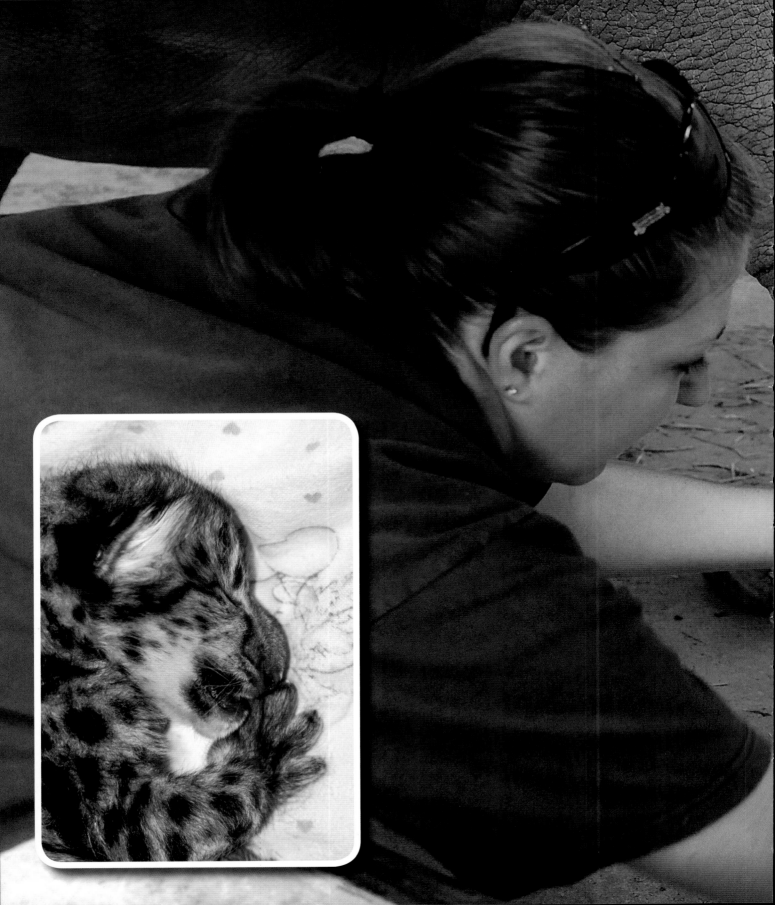

Would you help a newborn snow leopard find his paw or scrub a rhino's foot?

Could you build a new home for porcupines or rescue baby brown bears?

Would you create a cake for chimps and keep monkeys from becoming bored?

**Could you introduce baby chimps to their new troop or provide a snack for reptiles?**

keepers care for many different kinds of
nals. Some babies are born at the zoo.
nans, like this polar bear cub, may go back
e wild or be adopted by another zoo.

Keepers work closely with vets. Together, they give the animals vitamins to keep them healthy and medicine when they are sick. Keepers also train animals to hold still for check-ups and shots.

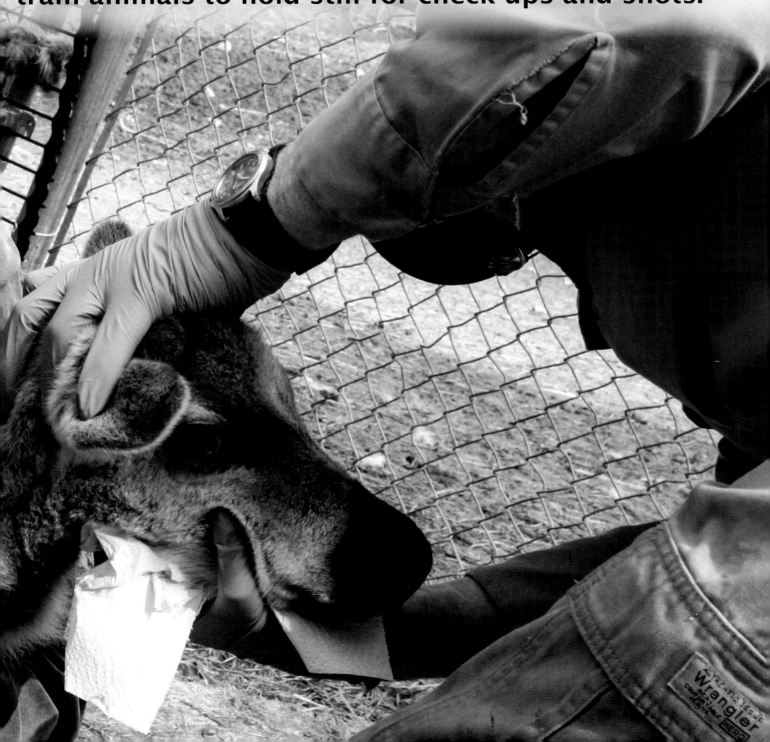

Like kids, animals hate to be bored. Keepers work with trainers and volunteers to create enrichment activities that keep the animals entertained and happy, like:

· a giant tractor tire swing for a chimp
· a splashing pool and ball for brown bears
· fake rocks for a cougar
· and a paper mache moose for wolf pups.

Zookeeping can be challenging. Zookeepers are always alert. Keepers don't often go inside the cages with the animals. Many animals are cared for from outside the cages. Training is an important part of a keeper's daily duties. Keepers train animals to "show" their paws, tail, and teeth, and to go "on and off exhibit."

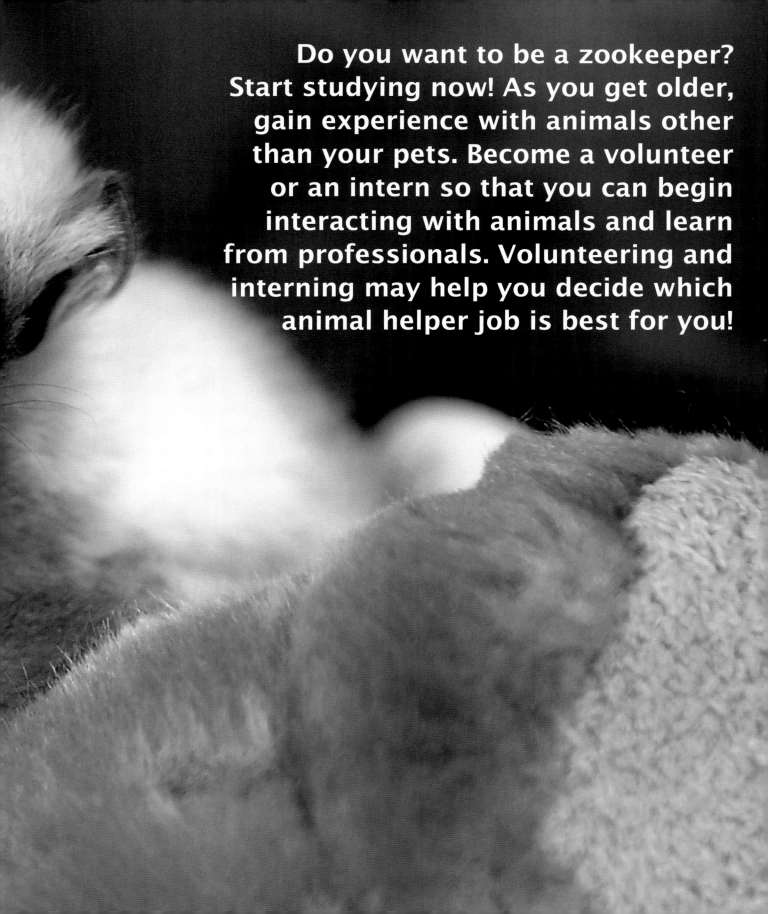

Do you want to be a zookeeper? Start studying now! As you get older, gain experience with animals other than your pets. Become a volunteer or an intern so that you can begin interacting with animals and learn from professionals. Volunteering and interning may help you decide which animal helper job is best for you!

# For Creative Minds

## Building a Zoo Habitat

Zookeepers work to provide animals in zoos with habitats best suited to their needs. All animals need space, food, water, and shelter, but habitats with these same four elements may look very different.

This Komodo dragon has plenty of space to move around and lots of objects for climbing. Do you think that a Komodo dragon needs more or less space in his zoo habitat than a giraffe?

A thick piece of meat is a tasty treat for this arctic fox. But, zoo animals don't eat the same meals. Who would eat a bale of hay: an elephant or a cheetah? Which animal do you think would rather eat fish: a seal or a chimpanzee?

Rhinoceroses love water. Rhinos drink the water and swim in it. Some animals need lots of water for swimming and playing. Others don't like water, except to drink. Who do you think needs more water in their zoo habitat: a lion or a polar bear?

A leafy tree provides shelter for this red panda. The thick leaves provide shade from the hot sun. Can you think of other kinds of shelters that different animals need in their zoo habitats? What does a lamb need? What does a bat need to roost?

Answers: 1: A Komodo dragon needs less space than a giraffe. 2: Feed the bale of hay to the elephant. Seals love to eat fish. 3: A polar bear needs lots of water to swim and to play. 4: Answers may vary. Lambs live in barns. Bats need caves or trees to roost.

# Wildlife Conservation

Some animals are at risk of becoming extinct. When a species becomes extinct, there are no more of that animal anywhere in the world. **Conservation status** indicates whether a species is at risk of becoming extinct.

Zookeepers help conserve and protect whole species through teaching, research, and breeding programs.

To keep local and exotic creatures safe, zookeepers offer "chats" to teach visitors about animals' habitats and threats. "Citizen science" programs allow people to gather data about issues affecting local species. For example, participants may count frogs in a certain pond. Volunteers may also work with the zoo staff to build or repair areas where animals can safely nest and find ways to help young salamanders or turtles safely cross roads.

Some zoos also work with experts to breed threatened or endangered animals. The babies are released into the wild or moved to different zoos to continue teaching visitors about the animals.

Zoos also support important conservation efforts worldwide. Some zoos raise money and work with organizations that provide habitats for animals to roam. They help hire guards to prevent poaching. Elephants, tigers, apes, and giant pandas are some animals supported by these zoos and organizations.

Some zoos rescue and care for injured or orphaned animals until they can be released back into the wild or another home may be found.

Many of the animals featured in this book are endangered and threatened, including: chimpanzee, colobus monkey, Coquerel's sifaka, cougar, polar bear, red panda, rhinoceros, snow leopard, and trumpeter swan.

## LC—Least Concern:
A species that is not currently at risk of becoming endangered.

## NT—Near Threatened:
A species that may become endangered in the near future.

## VU—Vulnerable:
A species that will soon become endangered unless people do something to change the situation.

## EN—Endangered:
A species in trouble. It may become extinct if people don't help.

## CR—Critically Endangered:
A species in dire trouble. It is likely to become extinct without immediate help.

## EW—Extinct in the Wild:
A species that only lives in captivity. The species still exists only because people take care of it.

## EX—Extinct:
A species we'll never see again. Extinction is forever.

trumpeter swan
Status: Endangered

chimpanzee
Status: Endangered

# True or False

1. Only exotic animals live in zoos.
2. Baby zoo animals may be fed through a bottle.
3. Zoo animals play with toys.
4. Some animals are born at the zoo.
5. Zookeepers teach tricks to the animals in their care.
6. Zookeepers want mother animals to care for their babies.
7. Keepers always go into adult animals' enclosures to care for them.
8. Zoos may serve as home for an orphaned animal until another home can be found.
9. In hot weather, zoo animals might snack on a Popsicle® or other icy treat.
10. Zookeepers are the same as zoologists.

1. False—All kinds of animals live in zoos. 2. True. 3. True. 4. True. 5. False—Zookeepers teach animals certain behaviors that make it easier to care for the animal, but they do not teach tricks. 6. True—Zookeepers want babies to be with their mothers in the zoo. 7. False—Zookeepers usually care for the animals from outside the enclosure. It can be dangerous to enter a cage with adult animals. 8. True. 9. True. 10. False—Zookeepers take care of the animals in zoos. Zoologists research and study animals in the wild and in captivity.

# Zookeepers, Zoologists and Veterinarians

Zookeepers and zoo veterinarians both care for zoo animals. They often work together to keep the animals healthy or to give them medicine if they are sick.

Zookeepers take care of exotic and native animals that live in the zoos. They might take care of one species or many animal groups: amphibians, birds, fish, insects, mammals, and reptiles. They prepare food, make sure the animals have plenty of water, clean cages, observe the animals, and help keep them healthy. They may design and build habitats, create enrichment activities, and help train the animals. Zookeepers may help raise the babies born in the zoo. They often work with veterinarians, other caretakers, and volunteers. They often take the lead in educating zookeepers and often answer questions during "Meet the Keeper" programs.

Zoo veterinarians are doctors who specialize in caring for the exotic and native animals that live in zoo settings. Veterinarians diagnose sick animals and prescribe medicine. They may operate on an animal.

Zoologists and wildlife biologists have a specific "animal science" college degree and may research and publish scientific articles about animals. Zoologists study where animals come from, sickness in animals, behavior, and their life cycle. Some zoologists collect data in animals' native environments to learn more about what affects the animals. Zoologists who study one animal group have specific names:

- Herpetologists study reptiles and amphibians.
- Ornithologists study birds.
- Mammalogists study mammals.
- Ichthyologists study fish.
- Entomologists study insects.

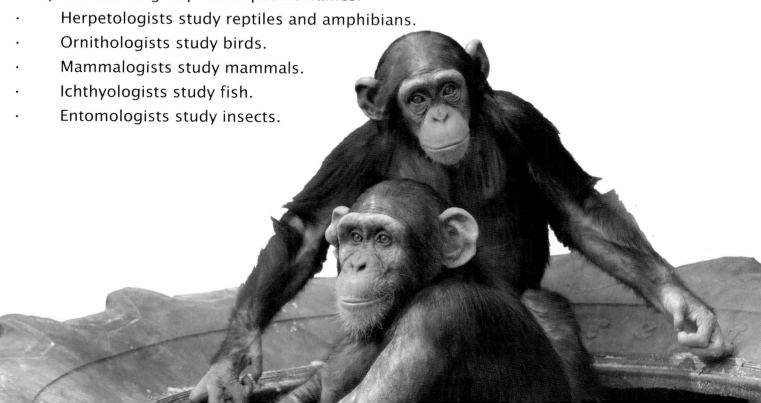

Thanks to the extraordinary experts with whom I've been working for their dedication and commitment to animals in need and for setting a wonderful example for our young readers. —JKC

Thanks to the following people and zoos for sharing their love of animals with us:
John Gomes and Patrick Lampi, Alaska Zoo, Anchorage, AK: www.alaskazoo.org
Patti Clark, Austin Zoo & Animal Sanctuary, Austin, TX: www.austinzoo.org
Jeff Bill, Robyn Johnson, and Carey Riccardone, Maryland Zoo, Baltimore, MD: www.marylandzoo.org
Brint Spencer and Jason Fantuzzi, Turtle Back Zoo, West Orange, NJ: www.turtlebackzoo.org

**Photo Credits:**

John Gomes, Alaska Zoo: Cover, trumpeter swans, moose, lamb, snow leopard, porcupines, brown bears, caiman, polar bear, caribou, wolf, FCM

Austin Zoo: FCM

Maryland Zoo: Title page, giraffe, rhinoceros, chimps, colobus monkeys, Coquerel's sifaka, FCM, imprint page

Turtle Back Zoo: red panda, cougar, FCM

Library of Congress Cataloging-in-Publication Data

Curtis, Jennifer Keats.
  Animal helpers : zoos / by Jennifer Keats Curtis with Patti Clark, Jason Fantuzzi, John Gomes, Robyn Johnson, Patrick Lampi, Carey Riccardone and Brint Spencer.
    pages cm.
  ISBN 978-1-60718-713-4 -- ISBN 978-1-60718-850-6 -- ISBN 978-1-60718-851-3 (ebook) -- ISBN 978-1-60718-852-0 -- ISBN 978-1-60718-853-7
1.  Zoo keepers--Juvenile literature.  I. Title.
  QL50.5.C87 2013
  591--dc23
                              2013021970

Animal Helpers: Zoos: Original Title in English
Ayudantes de animales: zoológicos: Spanish Title
Translated into Spanish by Rosalyna Toth

key phrases for educators: Environmental Education, jobs, threatened/endangered animals

Manufactured in China, June 2013
This product conforms to CPSIA 2008
First Printing

Sylvan Dell Publishing
Mt. Pleasant, SC 29464
www.SylvanDellPublishing.com